THINGS TO DO NOW THAT YOU'RE...A DAD

things to do now

DAVID BAIRD   Illustrations by Robyn Neild

that you're...
a dad

MQP

contents

introduction

Suddenly, after all the waiting and anxiety, fear and trepidation, word arrives. 'Congratulations! You are the proud father of….' It's possibly the biggest news you'll ever receive. Most of us drop our chins to our chests and think, 'What do I do now?' Some reach for cigars, others make phone calls, others faint…throw up…cry…run away…. There are as many reactions to this incredible news as there are new dads who receive it.

But we all have one thing in common…from that very instant onwards and for the rest of our lives…WE ARE DADS and any guy who has been a kid can be a GREAT dad.

If you were brought up without a dad or think you had a bad time with yours, then you'll know exactly what to add to a relationship between you and your own child to make it special and rewarding for you both. For others, who had the perfect relationship with the 'World's Greatest Dad', you can now share some of those memorable, life-shaping experiences with your own children and other dads who didn't.

The truth is that there are so many things you can do now that you are a dad!

those early days

> *Blessed indeed is the man who hears many gentle voices call him father.*

Lydia M. Child, *Philothea: A Romance, 1836*

Now is the time to relive those great moments you had with your own dad or to create one's you always wished you had had.

Fathers take note – it's not your method that is important, it's the results.

Think about this – what is it that you expect to do as a dad? Run through all the variations and make a list.

Find out what your child's mother expects you to take on as a new dad. This could be a good time to show her your list which miraculously has pre-empted most of her expectations of you. She will breathe a sigh of relief... and so can you.

Be a Dapper Dad.
Get some new clothes
and a trendy new haircut.

Act the part. You are, after all,
about to become a role model.

To a child, a loving father
is the most wonderful
person in the world.

*Whatever happens in the run
up to the birth, be prepared
to bite the bullet and hang in
there for your partner, after all
she's about to present you with
the greatest gift possible...
your child.*

*Inspire yourself with all the good things that
you want to do for your own children.*

Take great inspiration from what your father did for you.

Take inspiration from the things that you see other fathers doing with their children.

Be inspired and take heed of what your children want and need.

*Any man can be a father. It takes
some special qualities to be a dad.*

In your new role of father-to-be
try not to become either too
bossy or over-defensive towards
the staff at the hospital during
your baby's delivery. Trust their
experience and expertise.

At the hospital, if you must become a despot, then become a friendly despot.

Keep in mind that experiencing birth firsthand doesn't happen very often. Don't cut yourself off from the event by hiding behind technology such as cameras and camcorders.

During the delivery, dads-to-be should take a backseat. This is no time for control freaks to emerge.

It is accepted that you will be just as worried or scared as your partner, but the best thing you can do right now is look and learn. Keep your fears at bay with a doodle pad...it could be very revealing.

Now that you are a dad, make your visits to your partner and child in hospital reassuring. Your partner has been through a lot and her esteem may be dented. She needs to know that she is beautiful to your eyes and to your new baby. You are a family now, and you are the dad.

Keep things in perspective and don't become too pedantic. The nurses and midwives at the hospital deal with childbirth everyday. Sure, you attended a prenatal class and read the books, but they have the upper hand in this situation.

At the time of childbirth, don't steal the limelight. Be a new dad who will do whatever it takes to make mother and baby the stars of the moment.

A caring dad-to-be should help out in any way he's asked during the delivery. He'll gladly rub his partner's back and coach her in her breathing techniques. And may be if he's read-up on the situation he'll complete these missions without prompting.

Becoming a new dad gives one the immediate newfound freedom to express emotions – what better way than with a few tears of joy at the arrival of your new child.

The delivery room is a lesson for life – go with the flow.

Childbirth involves pain: your partner's not your own – unless you faint and knock your head on a bedpan.

Always keep a smile on your face and remain supportive to your partner, even in moments of stress and worry.

While you are still in the hospital your baby will be thoroughly examined by the paediatrician. Don't be afraid to ask questions.

If you intend to be constantly underfoot by visiting your partner pre-natal or post-natal, then don't forget the hardworking nursing staff with the occasional treat…some chocolates are always welcomed.

Be an on-the-ball dad-to-be. Do your homework and get to know the entire terminology ready for the big day and beyond. From epidurals to nursing bras – get yourself informed!

Once you get home from the hospital, be prepared for the fact that all babies produce a variety of bewildering and often unsettling sights and sounds – most of which are normal.

Start writing a journal. You don't have to be a professional to jot down a few events from each day or to chart the progress being made by your new arrival and the subsequent changes to yourself and family life. A journal is a great way to get in touch with your own feelings and makes for interesting reading in the years ahead.

Don't wait for your partner's instructions - learn to follow your own instincts of how to go about parenthood.

Dads, remember this: to a new child everything is new and for the first time! Things that may not amaze you any longer will certainly amaze them! Everything counts.

Fathers are not so different to mothers – both share concerns that their child has enough to eat and drink, has clean clothes and that they are entertained, safe and happy. So relax and enjoy the comfort you bring as a father.

Take time out to read up on a few of the basics of dealing with a baby. Know how to do certain things BEFORE your baby comes home...then show off!

Dedicate a bit of time to testing out temperatures so that you instinctively know if something is going to be too hot or too cold for your baby. Place a thermometer in the bath and get the bathwater to the right temperature. Feel it with your hand and elbow until you think you know when it feels right.

Communicate with the very young. OK, so they don't have a clue about language yet, but where do you think they pick it up from. Make lots of funny sounds and baby talk through play, but don't feel embarrassed to actually talk to them...it won't be long before they reply!

It only takes a few minutes to change a baby's clothes…? Don't worry, the entire process will become second nature in no time at all.

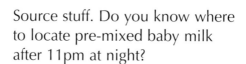

Source stuff. Do you know where to locate pre-mixed baby milk after 11pm at night?

Get used to burping, farting, blowing raspberries and squeals of laughter!

It is not advisable to feed your baby right before bath time.

It's natural to see many shades of green poo in almost every imaginable consistency being produced by your baby over the first few weeks and months – it doesn't mean you're raising an alien!

You won't be the first parent who finds that they check every few minutes to see if their baby is still breathing. According to experts, apparently we should expect fewer than 60 breaths per minute with occasional pauses that may last as much as six seconds – parents may also need to remember to keep breathing at stressful times!

When giving your baby a bath make sure the room is warm and that you have everything at the ready. Never, never, never leave your baby alone in its bath, even for a second.

Bath time should be a fun time. For stress-free tub time, make sure your baby is comfortable. Keep her well supported with your arm and be reassuring throughout. Remember to shield her eyes from any shampoo or soap and gently wash from tip to toe before rinsing and patting dry with a warm, soft towel.

Calm activities and a regular bath-time routine before bed can help prepare your child for a peaceful passage to sleep.

Babies will spit up – it's nothing to fret about. Try burping your child every few minutes during feeding, and if old enough, place the baby in an upright position in an infant seat or stroller right after feeding.

All children benefit from our participation. So get stuck in.

Suddenly after years of independence there is a helpless human being who is totally dependent upon you. That realization of responsibility is bound to wake you in the middle of the night.

There are going to be great physical and emotional changes in your lives and soon you can add sleep deprivation to the list – but one look in those baby eyes reminds you, 'I'm a dad…I'm a dad….' And on you go forfeiting another hour to bed.

It's important to look after all the family,
but you also owe it to yourself, and
them, to make sure you get enough sleep.
When baby naps, you nap.

*Try to take little breaks
during the day (and
let you partner do the
same). A short walk
can make the world of
difference...even doing
a few chores can be a
refreshing break.*

Take turns preparing dinner –
get into that kitchen and turn
on the radio. Relax and enjoy
this brief respite.

Just because you have new duties as the father of a new baby you can still achieve a great deal. Break your own projects into smaller, manageable tasks, then set about creating time each day to tackle one or two of them . . .you'll soon find a rhythm.

Invest in a Snugli baby carrier that allows you to work while carrying the baby strapped onto your front. They're fantastic and will allow your baby a whole new set of experiences while being in close contact with you as you walk, work or relax...together.

Get the most out of your visitors in those early days. Everyone can pitch in...they can even make you some lunch (and themselves, of course).

Greet unexpected visitors with 'You can either do the dishes and make a cup of coffee, or watch the baby while I do!'

Don't place all the thinking and remembering into the hands of your partner. Know when your baby was last fed or changed...know when he has his inoculations...double-check what has been packed in the car for a trip.

Never allow yourself or your partner to be affected by comments from friends or family about your parenting methods. It says more about their situation and emotions than it does yours.

Well-intentioned people are not necessarily right. Only accept advice that you know in your heart is likely to help with a particular situation, and above all else, trust yourself and your baby will trust her dad.

If you can weather the storms of the first weeks of fatherhood your reward will come in about six weeks time when your baby will recognize you properly as its father and give you a nice big gummy smile.

Learn the mantra – when there are two loving, caring parents, there will never be a wrong way or a right way of doing things...there will be two equally good but different ways.

It's a tough world out there and who better than a dad to show that it's possible to be gentle and caring within it.

No matter how short the time is that you get to spend with your child it is possible to develop happy father and child memories for you both.

In the mathematics of childhood, love equals dad's time plus attention.

One of the most important things a father can show his children is that he loves and cares for their mother. Even when they are very young, take them with you when you buy her flowers.

There's no pillow quite so soft as a father's strong shoulder.

Read to your children – starting from birth. It really helps to create a strong bond with them. Reading books can simply be looking at pictures or enjoying being together.

Make your home childproof and safe.

There are three stages of a dad's life: he starts out believing in Santa Claus, then he reaches a stage where he no longer believes in Santa Claus, then he becomes Santa Claus. Have you got your red suit and white beard?

It is vital for every dad to realize, and to do so quickly, that the greatest gift you can give to your children is your love. The only way to do this properly is by getting to know them and becoming involved in their lives so that they might also get to know you.

Now you are a dad, you can understand just what you put your own father through.

Now you're a dad, your perception of your life before children is going to change radically. What once seemed a hectic life will be an oasis of blissful calm. Don't worry, it will come back but not in a hurry.

Trust yourself. You are a loving and responsible parent and will do anything to ensure the wellbeing of your baby or child. Your ways may be different from those of your parents, and even your partner, but the goals are the same. . . a happy and healthy child.

Dads-to-be should see themselves as winners, not prove themselves to be whiners!

It is important for both you and your partner to get time alone during each day, if only to reassure yourself that you exist too!

embracing
your second
childhood

Perhaps most men fear becoming fathers because we aren't through being children ourselves yet. But fatherhood is the ideal doorway back to the nursery and an invitation to a second childhood.

It is well within your capabilities to bring creativity, fun, physicality and imaginative play into your child's world – so put on an eye patch and get swash buckling!

Time to dig out a few nursery rhymes and brush up on your singing skills. Don't be shy. Your child wants, and deserves, your voice...not a faceless voice from a box.

Get yourself a ukulele and learn a few chords. Your kids will love a sing-song with dad. Never played an instrument? Now's your chance.

Every Dad knows that the distance from your elbow to your wrist is about the same length as your foot and the length of your outstretched arms from fingertip to fingertip is roughly equal to your own height. Try it! This is stuff that will fascinate your kids.

Every child loves getting mucky, so now should you!

*Every dad should make a time capsule
with each of his children – it's fun and
informative and leaves a lasting legacy
to be handed down from generation to
generation. Fill a waterproof container
with photographs and newspaper
clippings, a few sacred mementos and
objects, and some sealed letters written
to each other with secrets or kind words,
then seal the whole thing. Place the
capsule to be unearthed sometime in
the future, unlocking it together and
flooding yourselves with fond memories.*

Make it a water day. Fill a tub or small pool with
water and find a variety of things that will float,
some that will sink and a few that can pour or
contain water. Be close at hand and watch as your
child experiments and discovers what the various
consequences of their actions will be. They may
get wet, but it's wonderful fun and a supreme
stepping off point into the world of physics.

Jump right in at the deep end, metaphorically speaking, and teach your baby or toddler to swim...the earlier the better as it will make it easier for him. It's great fun to join a group with an instructor where you get in the pool with your child. Think of the peace of mind it will bring.

Learn the gentle art of distraction. You'll need it if stuck in a traffic jam, waiting for a train or queuing at the supermarket checkout.

Mix 4 cups of flour and 2 tablespoons of salt with just enough water to make your own firm non-sticky play dough. Shape the dough into various forms, then bake them at about 150°C or 300°F for 2 hours or until dried out. Allow the items to cool, then paint.

Have an art day and make your very own Jackson Pollock painting (probably best done outside and on lots of coverings!) Set your blank paper either flat on the floor or upright against a wall or fence and drip paint onto it using various flicking and swirling motions. You'll be amazed at the results.

Before recycling paper, have a paper plane extravaganza. Get a book from the library or bookstore, or look online for designs of paper darts and planes and see how many different types you can fashion between you. Let your models compete with each other for duration of flight and distance flown.

Get yourselves along to a place where the water is broad and still, locate some small flat pebbles, and teach your children how to skip stones. This can occupy hours of time as each contestant becomes better and the number of skips increases – plus their is the endless search for new pebbles.

Relearn how to play
'I Spy With My Little Eye'
and other such car games –
play it with your partner before
the birth. . . it's just as fun and
engaging for adults.

'Knock Knock' and other jokes are an endless source of fun and amusement, and the cornier the better. Start stocking up on them now and you might just find enough to get you through a childhood.

'Knock knock...'
'Who's there?'
'Doctor!'
'Doctor Who?'

Why was the daddy glow-worm unhappy?

Because his children weren't very bright.

What's green and short and goes camping?

A boy sprout.

Did you hear about the boy
who kept stealing rhubarb?

*He was taken
into custardy.*

*When do kangaroos celebrate
their birthdays?*

During leap year!

What's the best way to
catch a monkey?

*Climb a tree and act like
a banana.*

Get some face paints and sit in front of the mirror with your child. Invent your very own clown face - it helps to have a book about clowns to hand for inspiration.

To avoid the usual tantrums associated with end-of-day tiredness, make bedtime something to look forward to each evening... it might be a story, a chat about the day or a snug and inviting bedroom environment.

It's important for every dad to know that bogeymen and monsters are all frightened of children and run away whenever kids go upstairs to bed!

Now you are a dad you can walk proudly down the street carrying a Barbie doll and have a valid excuse for doing so.

Get some luminous stars and planets and stick them on the bedroom ceiling. They will twinkle your child to sleep and take her mind off the darkness.

Now you can spend your hard-earned cash on toys for the boys - remote-controlled cars and skateboards...only please, do let them have a turn occasionally!

Now you're a dad you'll always have someone smaller than you to squirt with your water pistol!

Brush up on your round singing with songs like 'Row, Row, Row Your Boat', which can go on and on for ages and still be fun, especially during long car journeys.

Have a mud session. Visit a charity shop and search for a collection of utensils to use to make some mud pies in the backyard.

Summertime is the best time to source sleds cheaply! During the winter, dad's make the best sled pullers their children could hope for.

No dad should send his children down the helter-skelter at the fairground unless he is prepared to go down too!

Whether it's new or pre-loved, providing your child with a bike or scooter can give them a feeling of great independence – and you can teach them to ride it safely!

Family pool Olympics. Set out various races, games and challenges in the swimming pool and compete with your kids to score points, or better still, win prizes. Of course you should rarely, if ever, win any of the events yourself.

Teach your kids some of the little pocket games that are still available today at good toy stores such as pocket cricket, dice and jacks.

Too many dads see themselves as being in the thankless position of provider for all and also the enemy of all. These dads need a yo-yo and a ten-minute break with their kids!

Dads should be equipped with numerous suggestions for pastimes and fun projects to be undertaken on any occasion… they should be activities that will keep the children interested while helping them learn.

Now you are a dad you have an excuse to visit the amusement park and ride on that roller coaster you've always wondered about.

This may be hard, but from time to time allow your children to see that it is not the end of the world to embarrass yourself.

Model railways are great fun and relatively inexpensive – and if you look after them well some even increase in value over the years and can be passed on from generation to generation.

Buy a basic train set and mount it on a large board that can easily be slid beneath the bed and pulled out whenever it's a dull day.

It's possible to buy ready-made scenery and accessories for your model train set, but it's also great fun and rewarding to create your own using craft materials, plaster gauze and paint.

Become marvellous at marbles!

Learn the card games of 'Snap', 'Happy Families' and 'Go Fish'. When the kids have grown up, then you can fleece them at poker!

Go to a bridge and play Pooh Sticks. Drop your sticks in water over the upstream side of a bridge, then race to the other side to see whose comes out first! Great game Winnie!

Re-awaken all those old school playground games such as hopscotch.

Teach your children to whistle — if you can't do it yourself, try and learn together.

Introduce your children to things of your past. You could collect old comics that you read at their age, for example. They'll love it!

Who could possibly say they'd experienced childhood without having learned to play leapfrog? Bend over, tuck your head in and make a solid platform at a height your kids can vault over you.

Squash plants are perfect plants for a family gardening project. They are not costly and soon develop into impressive-looking vegetables.

Stand side-by-side looking in the mirror and pull funny faces for a few minutes of hilarious fun.

Every day the postman comes but rarely is there anything for the youngsters in the family. Why not occasionally pop something in the post for your children – a postcard, for example.

Keep cool when planning your children's parties. Try and think outside the box and a bit further than the ice cream and jelly experience of your day. Be adventurous! But don't go mad!

Get some balloons, some cut up old newspapers and some wallpaper paste and make papier maché masks. Cover the balloons with layers of the pasted paper, let it dry, pop the balloon and cut the mask to shape. Then paint!

Make and paint your own model figures with self-drying craft clay.

Pick a party theme kids will love – monsters, witches and wizards, cowboys or pop stars. Allow your child to help in the decision making as well as the designing and decorating of the room. It is his party after all and who knows what his age group likes better than him!

If you decide on a venue for a party that is not your home, then bear in mind size, space, ease of location, mess factor, cost and of course health & safety. Also, make sure you get there in plenty of time to set up and greet guests as they arrive.

Parties held at home are cheapest but do require lots of clearing up! If you are lucky to have good weather, the garden is always the best place, or if indoors, then stick to a particular area and define it with your decorations.

Help your child to design invitations. Make them eye-catching and include the vital information such as the time and address – sometimes a small hand-drawn map is useful. Children are busy people so send the invitations out in plenty of time.

A great cake is, of course, the finishing touch to any child's birthday party. You could go to the supermarket and buy one off the shelf or order a special one from your bakery. Better still, go right out on a limb and work with your child to design and bake one, with yourself accepting the consequences of the result.

An array of balloons and banners, streamers and table covers coordinated with your chosen theme will brighten up any party. Most party stores and supermarkets stock plates, napkins and party hats to fit a variety of themes.

Party bags are an art form in their own right these days. Some people go absolutely mad with these après-party handouts, while others throw in a hunk of cake and a balloon.

On birthdays and at Christmas your child will have received a pile of gifts – do try and make a note of what came from whom so they can send a thank you card afterwards.

When it comes time for your child to give gifts to others, encourage him or her to think imaginatively – making homemade gifts is both fun and personal.

Make some exotic fruity cocktails to refresh the party guests. Mix together various juices and fruits and have all the trimmings to hand – little paper umbrellas, cherries and olives on sticks.

Teach your children to give to the less fortunate – give charitable gifts. Make it a lasting gift. Send on behalf of each child a cow that enables poor farmers in Africa to become self-reliant, for example. The recipient will receive a card telling them about their gift.

Give toys that stimulate the senses.

Give gifts that promote active problem solving such as toys that involve seeking, solving, finding and researching. Puzzles, codes, construction games or science kits can be enjoyed by all the family.

Throw a themed birthday party every year – start with a kite party! Pocket kites are fantastic for little tykes.

Hold a teddy bear's picnic – find out when your children's bears birthdays are!

Children love and are fascinated by music. Whenever there is difficulty getting them off to sleep, make sure you have something soothing to hand. Better still, sing them to sleep yourself or lull them with some gentle instrumental playing if you are a musician...perhaps not a saxophone or timpani...but who knows!

Rediscover foods from your own youth while introducing them to your child.

Sharpen the family's eye co-ordination with a fun game of jacks. Throw the jacks on the floor, toss the ball from your hand into the air and try to pick up one jack with that same hand before the ball bounces once and you must catch it... then try picking up two jacks, three jacks and so on. Your turn continues until you miss the ball, miss the jacks, move a jack or drop a jack you've just picked up.

Teach your kids not to be frightened of animals by taking them along to a petting zoo where various tame animals await their visits and stroking them gently is positively encouraged.

Have endless hours of fun outdoors with pitch and toss. It's amazing how long these simple actions will entertain your offspring.

the great
outdoors

Every dad wants to bond with his kids. And while it's great fun going to the park followed by a hamburger the ritual can get a bit tiring. Seek some variation in routine.

Take your child out and about. Introduce him to the sky, the trees, the grass, the houses...in fact everything that he shares this world with.

THINGS TO DO NOW THAT YOU'RE...A DAD

It's up to you to propose activities that are fun and exciting for your kids. They will all be new and exciting to your children at the beginning, so they should be designed to be great relationship builders and, if possible, provide them with a useful skill.

Get a trampoline! Not only is it bouncing good fun but it will get you into shape while putting a smile on your child's face.

With some tape, a few sheets of polythene, some garden canes, a ball of string and some tissue paper any dull day can swiftly be turned into a kite-making day!

Remember what fun sack racing was as a child? Then why not find some large sacks and jump to it! Each person has to stand inside the sack and jump their way along a track to the finishing line.

Have a water war! Get lots of water in balloons, plastic bowls and buckets, water pistols and squirt guns. Then each team takes turns to sneak up on the other without getting absolutely drenched..., which of course, is impossible! This game is best played with a team of dads versus a team of kids on a hot summer day.

It's always fun to feed the ducks at the park.

Even dads can join in the three-legged-race! Standing side by side with your child and use an old necktie or piece of rope to lightly tie your two inside legs together. This means the pair of you must move as one 'three-legged' person…taking care not to trip up! It's all about rhythm and working together.

Why not have a wheelbarrow race against the stopwatch (dad inevitably is the carrier)? Get your child to lie on the ground on her front, and keeping her legs rigid, lift her from the ankles as though she were the handles of a wheelbarrow, except that instead of wheels she must walk on her hands along the track taking care not to collapse. This is best done on a lawn or soft ground.

Have a snowball fight.

Challenge your kids to see who can make the best snowman?

Get together and build an igloo in your garden.

If you have a small flat area of lawn, cut the grass and get out your croquet set.

Visit a Pick Your Own fruit farm and then make some jam together.

Go apple picking, then make a whole host of apple recipes: apple brownies, apple French toast, apple pie, baked cinnamon apples, caramel apple monsters, toffee apples or cinnamon apple chips.

A quick game to set up is volleyball. A bit of netting or even rope, stretched between two poles or trees, gives you the playing arena – a soft foam ball or beach ball is best if playing with young children.

Go out on a photo shoot! Most of us have some form of camera, and if not, they are so cheap there is no excuse – the memories they provide are priceless and last for generations. Capture each other on camera taking turns to be the photographer and have hours of fun afterwards looking through the photos.

If you are prepared to get stuck into a water fight, you can guarantee as much help as you wish when washing your car.

Never go on a picnic without a badminton set. It's amazing what fun and antics a couple of racquets and a shuttlecock can provide.

Frisbee golf is a great game that can be set up easily in a back garden or a park. Set some laundry baskets at a distance and perhaps place a flag on a stick beside them to mark out the golf course. Then, from a starting point throw frisbees trying to get them in the 'hole' in as few shots as possible.

Get hold of an old golf putter and golf ball. Bury a plastic cup or mug in the lawn and use your putter to hit the ball into the hole in as few strokes as possible.

Buy an old golf wedge, set up the paddling pool in the garden and take turns chipping the ball into the pool.

Try out the local driving range where
a bucket of balls can provide hours
of fun for father and
child as you take
turns driving
them at
targets.

*If you have a small flat area of lawn, cut
the grass and get out your croquet set!*

At some stage in every person's life they should experience the sheer exhilaration of rolling down a grassy bank. As you perfect your rolling skills, dads' can challenge sons and daughters to races. Always complete a thorough check of the ground for any sharp objects or mess before rolling.

Don't limit yourself to big name events. Take your child to experience local games, such as school football, hockey and rugby matches. He'll learn the rules and avoid the hype, plus, you'll save huge amounts of money to use for other things without sacrificing atmosphere or enthusiasm.

Dabble with the Diablo! It consists of a spool that is whirled and tossed on a string that is tied to two sticks held one in each hand.

Pack a picnic and together with some sketch pads and drawing implements, head off to the country, a lovely park, museum or ancient building. Come home having captured both of your impressions of your visit.

During the winter encourage your children to be helpful to wildlife. Build or buy a bird table, or hang a nut feeder, and charge your kids with ensuring there is food and water for the birds throughout the cold spells.

Kitchen table ornithology needs only a pair of binoculars and a bird-spotting book. Watch the bird feeder and log which birds come to visit.

After long, cold, winter walks, come home to a warm fire and thaw out with your child, drinking mugs of steaming hot chocolate with lashings of whipped cream and marshmallows!

Start a leaf collection. Collect great specimens and then, with your child's help, place the leaves between two sheets of wax paper, cover with a clean tea towel and press to keep them looking as fresh as the day you found them.

Create an obstacle course in the garden – things to hop over, climb, balance and cross.

Collect frogspawn in a practical and environmentally friendly way.

Create a worm farm.

If you have a family dog, seek out new and interesting places to take it for walks together.

Don't stop indoors just because it's cold outside. Grab the children, bundle them up warm and get out there. Focus the walk for any reluctant participants by collecting pine cones and things that will make good Christmas decorations later.

Set up a game of street hockey in a quiet street.

Get all of your children to bring their friends to the park and set up a big game of baseball or rounders – they'll learn the rules quickly and have a ball!

Keep the garden a clean, safe and fun place to play.

Encourage your children to examine plants carefully to see how they vary from each other.

'How do plants grow? Dad – you'll have to explain it!' Get reading – this will be just one of the hundreds of questions posed to you over the years.

You can easily tell a child whose dad has shown them what they can and cannot touch safely. These are the kids who don't run away when they see a worm or beetle – they are the ones who will pick them up, carefully examine them, then put them back from where they came.

Grow your own wood. For not too much money, or better still, splitting the cost with some friends, why not purchase a parcel of land and plant it with nature trees. In a few short years, your'll have a new and exciting play area.

Your children are not only great company in the garden, but also a useful spare pair of hands. Promise them their own plot in return for their help weeding or raking up leaves.

If you reward your child with a plot in the garden to call their own, use yours as the classroom. Teach him how to select seeds that will germinate quickly though, as every child is by nature impatient and will be hoping for results by tomorrow.

Dads who enjoy radishes will enjoy the fact that they are very child-friendly plants, as they will pop their heads up in just a week! Likewise, marigolds are rewarding – bright orange and easy to grow.

Teach your child the value of food by encouraging him to sow plants that not only look impressive, but can also be eaten!

Runner beans are a must for all young gardeners as they have pretty red flowers before the beans appear, which of course taste delicious when cooked.

Make some window boxes during spring and early summer – simple troughs that can be painted and planted with easy-to-maintain flowers.

Every garden should have a wheelbarrow. It not only makes light work of shifting heavy objects, but also provides hours of entertainment for youngsters, as they sit inside them, holding tight, while dad runs them around the garden! Thrilling stuff!

Be a thoughtful dad – kids like to pitch in and try their hand at grown-up tasks. Provide a child-sized (bought or cut down to size) broom, rake, spade and bucket so they can 'lend a hand'.

Teach your children the benefits of composting and how it becomes the nutrition for the soil.

During hot spells plan a watering rota for the garden between you and your kids.

Make someone 'in charge' of the weather. It's their job to search the newspaper, Internet, TV or radio for the day's weather report and present it to the family over breakfast.

After teaching your kids, with the help of a book, what stings and what bites, set them loose on a bug hunt to discover as many varieties as they can see, logging each one in a book as they find them.

In autumn, there's a great deal of fun to be had simply sweeping up all the leaves into a big pile and then letting the kids leap through and tunnel beneath them.

Let the children who are old enough make a log-pile that will be useful for the winter months, and also creates an environment where small creatures can go when it's cold.

Everybody plant a tree and take responsibility for its wellbeing. If things go wrong, simply plant another!

Have a sunflower growing competition.
Plant some sunflower seeds next to growing
canes with your names on them, and mark
each plant's height as it grows, making the
measuring a daily or regular event. Keen
competition makes for keen measuring – all
good for school.

*Join a local voluntary conservation
group as a family and become
engaged in a variety of
environmentally friendly activities.*

*Get the beach towels out in
the garden and let the kids sit
on them out in the fresh air.
Make sure they are wearing
a high factor sun block.*

Have a garden beach party. On a hot day, put up a garden umbrella, have your children wear swimsuits and put out some beach balls, frisbees and seashells. Get out the paddling pool or the sprinkler for them to run through and cool off.

If you have a sand pit, why not bury secret treasures in it, dress like pirates and go dig it up!

Stuff some old clothes with leaves and make a loveable scarecrow for the garden.

Try to build a bird's nest using only materials a bird might use.

If you have access to a chestnut tree, then why not pass on your skill at playing conkers?

For quiet evenings together with your children, why not introduce them to model making. There are thousands of affordable kits available in shops and online for dinosaurs, planes, ships…you name it! There'll be glue and paint everywhere – just lay out enough newspaper to protect the floor and you'll have nothing to worry about.

Have a treasure hunt.

Think about fun ways to raise awareness of environmental issues. Encourage children to consider their impact upon the world around them with gifts such as nest boxes, binoculars, bird feeders or gardening sets.

Get active with the camera and encourage your children to do the same. Start a big photograph album and make sure you feature in it as well, not just the kids.

rainy day fun

Rainy days are days to dream of sunnier times. Get out sheets of paper and crayons and sit with your children to draw a plan of how you want the garden to look. This is a great time to plan the kinds of plants you would like to grow.

Play on some loud morning music. What better way to start the day and get everybody into gear than some rousing music to stir them from their beds...if you can play the bugle yourself...even better!

Speaking of rhythm, why not get hold of a few drums, or even make them, and with the kids, experiment with a bit of tribal drumming in the comfort of your front room?

Introduce the game of Paper, Scissors, Stone – it can fill any dull moment.

Be pampered for a day in your daughter's beauty salon.

Grow to love jewellery made out of pasta!

It is time to refresh your memory of good old playground games you can teach to your children and here are a few to get you going:

Teach the kids to play Blindman's Bluff – a blindfolded person tries to catch someone else in the room. The person caught then gets blindfolded for the next round. .

Purr like a kitten after completing a game of Cat's Cradle – you'll need a length of string tied at the ends to make a circle – look online for instructions on how to play.

Sleeping Lions – all players lie down on the floor, eyes closed and are 'lions'. One player is the hunter and must move amidst the lions trying to make them move or make a sound by telling jokes and other means. This must be achieved without touching them. Any lion who moves, stands up and joins the hunter.

Follow the Leader – a leader moves about and all must do exactly as he or she does. Any who mess up are out of that round and the winner is the last player remaining who is not the leader.

Bulldogs – one or two players are selected as bulldogs to stand in the middle of the play area. All players stand at one end of the area then run to the other, trying not to be caught by the bulldogs. If they are, they become a bulldog themselves. The winner is the last surviving runner.

Musical Chairs – The game starts with a number of chairs – one fewer than the number of players – arranged in a circle facing outward. While music plays the players dance around the island of chairs. When the music suddenly stops, everyone races to sit down on one of the chairs. The one left without a chair is out. Another chair is removed and the process, repeated until the winner is the only player on the last remaining chair.

Teach your children some clapping games such as:
Pat-a-cake, pat-a-cake, baker's man.
Bake me a cake as fast as you can.
Pat it and roll it and mark it with 'B'
And put it in the oven for Baby and me.

There are so many knots on offer yet when it comes to the crunch most of us know very few, and the ones we do know are often unsuitable for the task. Get several lengths of rope and a good book and see how many different knots you can master between you.

A bowline is a commonly used knot to form a loop that neither slips or jams. Make a small loop and pass the free end of the knot up through the loop, around behind the standing part of the rope, and back down through the loop. Use this handy rhyme to teach your child – 'the rabbit comes out of the hole, round the tree, and back down the hole again'. The hole is the small loop and the rabbit is the running end of the rope.

Ever played Sardines? It is a bit like Hide and Seek... one person finds a hiding place and hides, the others try to find the hider and hide with them cramming into even the tiniest of spaces... hence sardines! The last to find all the others hiding becomes the hider in the next round.

Get hold of some acrylic paints. They are brilliant to have around, as they cover huge spaces and dry in half an hour. The shades and tones available are fantastic and everything washes out with water!

Make some jack o' lanterns. All you need are big pumpkins, something to draw on them with, a knife (which you'll be in charge of until the big handover when they are the right age), and a spoon for hollowing out the pulp and seeds. Carve a friendly, spooky face on each pumpkin and pop in a nightlight or small candle. Trick or Treat!

Put the scooped-out seeds aside and plant in the spring and watch your jack o' lanterns come to life.

Go to a local stamp collectors shop where you'll be able to buy a huge bag of stamps quite cheaply. Mount them in and album and wait for a rainy day to sit down with your child and discover the world through its postage stamps. Sometimes, the hobby can become quite lucrative as precious stamps turn up. It's a collection that will never stop growing even when your children do.

Learn the pea and shell trick. Which shell is it under?

Experiment with different smells and maybe make some nice smelling perfume using flower petals and water.

Make up a great collective story. Sit in a circle with your children and take turns adding one paragraph to the story. Will it ever end? Too short? Start another!

Grow some bean sprouts and watercress on the kitchen windowsill.

Matinee movies are a fantastic way to fill a wet or dull day with a few hours of escape in a multi-million dollar adventure in comfortable surroundings.

Whenever there's a quiet spot in the family calendar, make tracks for your local museum.

It may rarely have featured on your itinerary before becoming a dad, but there is nothing as spectacular for kids and adults alike as a good ballet or opera production.

Make a recorded message for the future – hear those young voices and just feel the memories come flooding back years later.

How about some secret agent activities?

Learn how to write and send messages. Try using invisible ink. Simply take a quill or ink-free fountain pen nib and write your message using lemon juice. It will look invisible to the naked eye, but by gently warming the page (under adult supervision) over a candle flame the juice will brown and the message will appear.

Why not create, or better still, learn an existing form of sign language that you can use to speak to each other in secret.

Invent a special secret code of your very own. There are plenty of samples available online, but a good one is to write words simply using the letter that falls after each letter in your word – so that WORD becomes XPSE...(ipx't uibu!)

Great for times of power cuts or simply when the right moment arises, use your darkened room as the stage for some magical hand shadows. Using a torch or candlelight, take turns to create various shapes on the wall with your hand and see if the others can guess what they are.

Every power cut can be turned into good fun when you have a few flashlights at hand. Use the time to play a game of flashlight hide and seek around the house or invent other games – such as flashlight sniper. The 'sniper' has the flashlight and stands with his back to the other players who try to sneak up on him. If they get caught moving in the beam when he turns around, they are sent back to the starting point.

Weather out stormy weather together by concentrating on it and passing on tales of great historical storms. If you don't know of any, search some out from books or the Internet, or better still, imagine even bigger storms and invent a story around them until the sun comes out again.

THINGS TO DO NOW THAT YOU'RE...A DAD

Show off your heirlooms. Have each member of your family bring out a few of their prized possessions and share stories about them.

Unearth your home movies and watch them as a family.

Turn any stranded moment into thrilling fun. A couple of drinking straws and a rolled up piece of paper napkin can easily be turned into a tabletop blow-football tournament, which will help you wait for the clouds to pass on a wet seaside holiday.

Encourage your children and their friends to make up plays and have them perform them to the parents at the end of the play-making session. Be prepared to spend the hours that follow putting the house straight again.

We've all seen custard pies thrown in movies, but why not stage your own? Get a pile of paper plates and some shaving foam, and run riot holding a pie fight!

Every family should have a go at karaoke at least once. You could even invest in a karaoke machine of your own and bring it out on dull, wet weekends and during seasonal celebrations.

Popcorn is not just for the movies. It will perk up any drab afternoon.

Hold a gurning competition once a year and give an annual prize for the ugliest face anyone can pull...don't forget to take photos.

Step up in the world on a pair of stilts! Knock up a pair of stilts from two shoulder-height lengths of wood with blocks attached firmly to them to be stood on at a height that isn't too scary for your child or dangerous.

Make up some pocket-sized parachutes with a square of light fabric or handkerchief, a small weight as the 'pilot' and four short lengths of string.

Movie making has become something within reach of most of us now with the advent of domestic video cameras and digital recording. Try the second-hand market for older cameras that use video tape, as you can pick one up for a fraction of its original cost. Write up a shooting script together and go off and make your mark.

Spend an hour together exploring the dictionary. Challenge your children to find words beginning with different letters of the alphabet, then get them to read out the meanings.

Plan an aquarium and study fish keeping – when ready, make it happen and take care to look after it.

Why not learn to bake your own bread to go with some homemade jam.

See what circus skills you can work on safely together at home, and when perfected, put on your very own circus show for family and friends.

Put on some music and invent a new dance.

Please yourselves with poetry. Why not hold a family poetry competition or festival with prizes and certificates.

Frame newly written poems, photos of winning sunflowers and special pieces of art, and display them proudly.

Spend a day researching the family tree – it's quite easy to do online.

Get a big, clean jar and cut a slot in the lid that is big enough to be able to insert coins. Encourage your children to save any spare coins (and top the jar up yourself occasionally). Empty them out once a month, count them up, then cash them in around Christmas or holiday time and do something nice with the savings!

Record yourselves reading a ghost story like a radio broadcast and make the sound effects to go with it. It takes a bit of preparation and forethought, but is great fun to do.

Never throw out old socks – with some scraps of cloth, a couple of buttons and a rainy day, there's a sock puppet character in each one of us just waiting to be born!

Teach older children the game of darts. A great pastime that both kids and adults, with a steady throwing hand can participate in.

When it comes to holding your breath, try to learn circular breathing with your children. Use a drinking straw and a glass of water, and breathe in through the nose and out through the mouth without breaking the flow. Master this and you'll be able to play the Didgeridoo!

Set up what some call a French football or table football set. It only takes a small amount of space and provides hours of thrills and spills.

Cover a tea tray with small objects (approximately 20), then give the contestants 30 seconds to study and try to remember them. Then cover the tray with a cloth and see how many objects they can recall in 30 seconds.

Beginning at one end of a long, thin cardboard tube, push nails shorter than the diameter of the tube through its walls. Place the nails a couple of fingers apart, and make a spiral pattern as you move along the tube. Block off one end and pour in a couple of handfuls of popcorn kernels, little shells or gravel, then seal the other end and invert. You've created a rainstick!

*Take 2 teaspoons milk, 3 scoops
chocolate ice cream, 2 tablespoons
chocolate syrup, 5 tablespoons
powdered chocolate drink mix,
5 cubes ice and a handful of
chocolate chips and process for
30 seconds in a blender. You've
created a chocolate chip milkshake!*

Write a pop song.

Get a short bamboo pole and attach a string to
it with a small magnet at the end. This is your
fishing rod. Behind a cloth screen (a blue sheet
will do nicely) lay some paper cut-outs of fish
on the floor, each with a small metal strip or
washer attached, then try to catch them.

Organize a family game of charades where a player acts out a fictional character, such as Scrooge, Rudolph, Santa, the Grinch, Widow Twanky, while the audience try to guess who they are!

Bake a gingerbread house and decorate it with ready-made squeeze-on icings.

Cut some starfish, fish and crab shapes out of sponge for the children to play with in the bath.

Bring out the glitter and spend a wet-weather day making your Christmas cards.

Make some shadow puppets. Hang a sheet in front of a light source, and from behind the screen, move abstract shapes or cutout figures to present a play. These can be as elaborate as you desire, with moving limbs and rodded movements – look online for ideas.

Cut a potato in half, then cut a relief pattern into the flat side. Dip in, or brush on, paint and press on paper to make a print. Cut holly or Christmas tree shapes to make great wrapping paper and Christmas cards.

Get a book or visit an origami website. You'll find loads of paper folding projects – one is the water bomb, which has several hilarious applications once you know how to make it.

Why not create a website of your new family, either for yourselves and friends with coded access or for the whole world to see and participate in?

In terms of games for the imagination, there's no better toy to have in a home than a big trunk filled with clothes for dressing up, procured from your local thrift store.

Find two empty and clean food cans with the lids safely removed and no sharp edges. Using a hammer and nail, punch a hole into the bottom of each can. Put the bottoms together and tie a large knot in one end of a piece of string and feed it through the two holes. Tie a knot in the other end, then pull the string tight between the two cans. Try various lengths of string from arm's width upwards. One person speaks into one can while the other listens into the other end…you've made your very own tin can telephone!

Cut a potato in half. Scoop out the middle and replace with cotton wool. Dampen the cotton wool and sprinkle on grass seed, which will grow very quickly! The end result looks like a hedgehog!

an awfully big adventure

Encourage your children to explore the world and find out about new things to do and try.

Visit a new country. Having children is a great excuse to travel – it is educational and mind expanding. Of course, you can revisit countries you've already seen, but why not discover ones that are new to you and your child?

Visiting castles and battlefields, museums, seaside towns, working farms and exhibitions will not only create great long-term memories for you both, but will also play a vital part in the development of your child's curiosity, encourage his imagination and stimulate the senses.

Pony trekking is one of those easily attainable pastimes that can turn a day out into a lifetime adventure for you and your kids to cherish.

Take the family out to sample the thrills of stock car racing or demolition derby and have a smashing time!

These days with Internet auction sites, junk and charity stores, it is easy and inexpensive to pick up good quality camping equipment. Gear up and take the kids on an adventure…camping sites are scattered all over the world.

Plan with your children a number of weekend and holiday outings aiming to experience as many different types of transport – from steam to air, and cycling to hot air balloons.

Don't shy away from exploring your own country - take your children on trips that will help them understand their own country and customs, traditions and folklore.

Every dad should spend at least one night out with his children exploring the wonders of the night sky. All it takes is a warm, dry night, a flashlight, a flask of hot chocolate, a couple of sleeping bags and a book to cross-reference what you see. Look out for shooting stars and don't forget to wish.

Get on your bikes and go off on an expedition with the kids – of course, taking lashings of lemonade and buns!

Try some outdoor pursuits. During the summer, head to a supervised lake where you and the kids can hire a canoe (and life jackets).

Seek out an indoor rock-climbing wall where all the equipment is supplied and dads can take turns belaying their kids and being belayed by them.

Turn your indoor rock-climbing training into the real thing and enrol on a supervised outdoor course designed to take you to the level you and your children seek to achieve.

*Put on your backpacks
and go hiking.*

Spend a day at the seaside and work together
as a team to create the perfect sandcastle.
Agree on who is in charge of what duties…
locating sticks for flagpoles or seashells for
adornments, and take turns forming the
battlements. Develop a story about your
kingdom as you go along.

Get a metal detector and go out in search of buried treasure. Roughly ploughed fields and beaches are good areas to find things.

Teach your kids pool safety – to always have an adult at hand and never to swim alone; not to throw people in or chase around the pool deck; and to always check the depth before diving in.

Have a go at roller-skating or roller-blading in a park, or other suitable areas where such things are tolerated.

Teach your children to snorkel. Once they master how to breathe with their faces under water, a whole new exciting world of wonders awaits them in the sea.

Seek out a forest aerial assault course. It's not dangerous if you follow the instructions, but not for the faint hearted. Your children will have fantastic fun while learning the importance of safety checks.

Go on a camera safari – shooting pictures of all the animals you see.

If you are an environmentally-friendly dad, then take your kids on an emissions-free, offshore yachting adventure.

Pit yourself against your offspring in a paintball battle – seek out a local organization.

Why not experience the sport of kings and go to a bird of prey park where you can learn to fly hawks for a day.

You'll need a lot of kit and a pocketful of courage to set out on an extreme wilderness survival weekend, but it's certainly character building.

Take the children ice-skating at a local ice rink. If none of you can skate yet, book a teacher for an hour – it'll be well worth it.

Get go-carting!

For excitement, there's nothing quite like going to the horse races as spectators. If you must bet, do so between each other for chocolate or sticks of gum, and be sure to soak in the electrifying atmosphere.

Shoot through fast-moving rapids, bounce off rocks, and speed in and out of eddies and icy pools on what looks like an inflatable armchair...try river bugging! Alternatively, seek out your closest white water rapids.

Field archery is an underestimated and challenging skill for all ages – either static targets or shoot on the move, flying your arrows at non-living targets.

At any height nothing beats the sound and exhilaration of viewing the world below from the basket of a hot air balloon.

Imagine the surface of the water
being broken and there she blows.
Take the youngsters whale watching!

There are many places around the
world where it is possible to pop on
a wetsuit, mask and snorkel and swim
with seals. Seek one out on your next
family holiday.

Whether there's snow
or you are on a rig with
wheels, racing through
forests and woods behind
a team of dogs on a
sleigh is an unforgettable
experience.

For those unlikely to enjoy skiing down mountains, why not try cross-country skiing, which is the original way of man getting about on skis–and you can stop anytime you like to take in the view!

Travel to inner space by taking a caving or potholing course. Always do this under supervision.

Successful beachcombers do a walk at low tide, noting the high tide marks where debris has been deposited along the beach, then they return just after the following high tide to begin combing the beach for shells and other treasures washed ashore.

Take to the snowy heights and have a crack at glacier skiing.

Tough work for you and older children? Yes? Why not try ice climbing? It is extremely challenging but not for the unfit. Your axe and crampon points bite into the surface of a near vertical ice wall when hopefully your will power and fitness will do the rest.

Spend some time learning winter skills and survival techniques for cold conditions. Make the highlight the preparation of a snow hole, and camp out overnight inside it!

When your child reaches a certain age, and before you become too old, why not do something extraordinary together like chartering a flight in a Russian MIG jet to the very edge of space?

Experience zero gravity – it's popular now and sold commercially, and if you don't like heights you can do it from the ground at various locations in a vertical wind tunnel.

Experience life with the Bedouin in Jordan and Egypt on a specialist adventure holiday.

Tree houses are not difficult to construct, and can become the stage for many hours of imaginative play and fun, a place of solitude or a home away from home.

Twilight is the perfect time for outdoor games, especially if you have access to a wooded area or park.

Make two teams (your kids, their friends and even their parents, if they are about). Each team places their flag in a secret place, then both teams try to capture the other's flag. Members of the opposite team can also be captured and held prisoner at base until freed by being tagged by a member of their own team.

Perfect your juggling – start with balls and move on to clubs.

Put on a firework display, following all the guidelines for safety.

Get your skates on! Turn the backyard into a skating rink. Flatten the snow and sprinkle layers of water on top, letting each layer freeze before sprinkling again and again until a thick ice surface has formed.

Do something together for charity–dress up or go on a sponsored walk or bike ride.

Visit a glass-blowing factory.

A fishing rod and reel costs very little – get your hands on some bait and find somewhere to fish (you may need a permit for this). This is best done in sunshine, with a picnic, and while you teach your youngsters how it's done it's an excellent opportunity to catch up and get to know each other better.

Collect fossils on the shoreline.

Fishing is not only a wonderful way to pass a few hours together with your child, but also passes on an understanding of survival and preservation.

Have a canal boat holiday or just ride as passengers for a day. Explain how the locks work, and even operate them together.

Dedicate one night a year to an all night UFO spotting session. Psyche up by reading about the latest UFO sightings and visiting dedicated websites.

What better way to get to know your community than to be tourists in it for a day and discover everything you can about it? Pop into the church and really have a good look at its design and stained glass windows... in some churches you can even do brass rubbings with paper and crayons.

Make pop bottle rockets and watch them soar! You'll find instructions on lots of websites.

Download some plans, get out the tools, and build a go-cart with your kids.

Be braver than you have been ever before. You are somebody's dad.

the learning
curve

Stimulate a child's mind and you will permanently boost their brain function.

Now you are a dad you can experience the thrill of leadership. Remember, always inspire…never boss!

A sensible dad will try to make everything they wish their child to do as enjoyable an experience as possible, never something to dread.

A dad should be prepared to accept that his children could open his eyes to entirely new possibilities.

Children don't like things that are too difficult or too frightening, and they will often switch off to them. Keep an eye out for any obvious signs of distress, and step in with a change of scenery.

Spend an hour exploring balancing things.

Consider owning a pet –
from a stick insect to a
Saint Bernard – pet ownership
teaches responsibility and
provides friendship
and understanding.

Introduce your child to the concept of 'a place for everything and everything in its place' by getting him to help you sort out the shed or tidying up the bookshelves while arranging the books alphabetically.

Kitchen experiments are great fun. Get out a bunch of different foods, and together with your youngster, try them all. You go first. Your reactions will most likely be mimicked by his so make sure you 'like' all the good nutritious things you want them to like!

Dads must be able to entertain and educate. Younger children will want to see a trick performed over and over again, while older kids will want to learn how to do it themselves.

Make your kids want to seek your help with homework by being clued up on topics that you know they struggle with.

Make school less of a chore by helping your child to prepare the night before for the day to come.

Don't forget playtime. Parents tend to worry exclusively about their children's homework and not focus on quality down-time. Time with a loving parent, slotted between the slog of scholastic activity, is a great motivator.

Stimulate your student. Invent some lesson-based games – translate a pie chart into baking, then eat the real thing!

Play with your children. Fathers often enjoy active and tumble play and children can learn a lot from this sort of play with their fathers. They learn that you can be strong and have fun while still being gentle, always stopping before things get out of hand.

Bedtime is a great opportunity to begin introducing all those classic stories, such as Peter Pan, into your child's life. Set the atmosphere…

Politeness should begin at home – the way we are with our children will influence the way they are towards others as they grow up.

Put on your 'TAHITI HAT' and ponder some palindromes.

Teach perseverance. Encourage your children to stick at a problem even if it is hard.

Many a lesson has been passed on from father to child while playing catch with a ball in the garden or park.

Learn a new language. Young minds are like sponges and pick up new languages easily alongside their native tongue and so too can you…take lessons together.

Spend a day measuring and comparing – all you need is a tape measure and some paper and pencils. It's a great way to introduce the notion of exploration, discovery and recording to your children.

Pass on some of your accumulated knowledge. If you are up on the classics, introduce a brief synopsis to your children. Kids love mythology and epic tales.

Introduce your children to the stories of Shakespeare before they are confronted with the text that can sometimes put young people off.

Teach your children about rules and laws. Teach by your actions, as well as what you tell them. Stick to what you believe is right and in their interests, even if it annoys them.

Invite new friends and their children over for dinner parties. Set up two tables – one for the grown-ups and a smaller one within eyesight for the youngsters, so that they might pick up good socializing skills from you and you can keep an eye on them from a safe distance.

Help save the planet! Get a recycling routine going and give all the family members equal responsibility. Make a trip to the local recycling amenity and unload your hoard to be put back into good use.

Become friends to something important... adopt a zoo animal and sponsor its wellbeing... join Friends of the Earth... plant a tree and nurture it.

Don't be fooled into thinking that children learn more from what we say than what we do – they analyze our every action and reaction in detail and often mimic us in their own ways when faced with similar situations.

Encourage your children to play board games and tackle challenging puzzles, as these will increase their analytical and strategy-forming skills.

Let your child bond with the family dog at dog handling classes.

Enjoy your children's company and do things together. Get involved, read, play, have fun!

Learn the different flags of various nations; make cards of them (putting the answers on the back); and test which you and your kids can remember. Add the capital city for interest

Children moan when they are bored… just like their dads! Help them to find a hobby they'll enjoy for a lifetime. Make a list and see what lights their fuse!

Share your own interests and hobbies with your children by involving them in what you do.

Help your children with sporting or hobbies they enjoy by attending their games and maybe even coaching or helping out with their team.

Show your kids how not to get electrocuted – make sure they know to not try and rescue the burning toast from the toaster with a knife!

Remember to set an example of how and where to safely cross the road.

Don't eat potato chips in front of your youngsters when you want them to concentrate on carrot sticks and apples!

Art is a wonderfully absorbing and creative pastime to hand on to your children wherever you chose to do it.

Surround your children with art materials. Let them get messy and get them to start thinking spatially and creatively at the same time.

Books will help your children develop their language and communication skills. For reluctant readers, help them choose books that you know will keep them engaged.

As your child's spatial awareness develops, offer her toys and projects that have a strong element of construction to them.

Fill your home with musical instruments or at least musical toys so that you can help children develop an understanding of rhythm and pitch.

Don't always feel the need to interfere with children who simply wish to play alone. Solo play can help stimulate their intellect and is a form of play akin to science.

Sooner than you think your child will announce that they have a driving licence, so set good driving examples yourself now. Avoid bad habits and speeding and try to control your road rage.

Driving is like swimming, better learnt young, and with experience these skills can be lifesavers not life-takers. Teach your teen to drive. Ask parents who have done this to talk you through their experience.

*Every home should have a
magic set.*

*Get a guitar and teach yourself
the 12 bar blues! Then teach
your child and JAM!*

Let your kids know that it's
perfectly OK to have their own
way of thinking and doing
things, and that they don't have
to do everything the way you
do or for the same reasons that
you do them.

*It is important for your children
to understand that they can be
independent individuals and to
know that you like them as they are.*

For those dads who want their children to be a credit to them, learn now that the fundamental defect with fathers is that they want their children to be a credit to them!

You can always recognize a generous dad. When he opens his wallet there's only pictures of his kids where the money should be!

By the time a man realizes that maybe his father was right, he usually has a child of his own who thinks that he's wrong.

Relax…what your children become will rest less with what we try to teach them than what they learn from us over the years at odd moments when we aren't trying to teach them anything at all.

There is an old saying that every dad should keep at the front of his mind: 'Never raise your hand to your kids. It leaves your groin unprotected!'

It is a great moment in life when a father sees his child grow taller, stronger or reach farther than he. Log all changes and achievements.

Don't be afraid to develop your own style of playing, teaching and nurturing your child. It may differ from that of your spouse, but dad's way is extremely valuable to your child too.

The role of dad goes well beyond that of minister for fun. For there is no need in childhood as strong as the need for a father's love and protection.

What a father says to his children is not heard by the world, but echoes in posterity

Teach the hard lessons of gambling by having a home casino game. Nobody likes it when they are losing, but your children need to learn that everybody can lose at some point.

Encourage children to make a note of their thoughts and keep a notebook handy for your own too.

Allow your children to see and understand your passion in life, whether it is football or music, art or movies.

How can a father possibly illustrate for his son how he should be when he becomes a man if he does not allow the son to spend any time in his company and that of other grown men? Even a trip to a football match with a few sons and their fathers will set an example.

Kids love it when their dads take them to their place of work. If you can't manage it during working hours, then why not pay a special visit out of working hours.

A tour of dad's workplace and a demonstration of what it is he actually does can promote a far greater understanding between father and child.

Show your child an empty space at your workplace and then when you get home ask for a special piece of artwork to be created to hang in it.

Give your child the chance to experience little work scenarios. Set up an office desk with pencils, phone, paper clips, etc. and ask them to do little office-like tasks for you such as stapling documents together neatly.

You don't have to send your teen off to work in the mill to teach them to have a healthy attitude towards money and how to appreciate it. Instead, show them how to manage their money well by budgeting and putting aside funds for a rainy day.

There's no point in providing a top notch phone if you never get a message or call from your child, and they use it simply to prank about and message friends. Try to discuss with them the appropriate use of such devices rather than simply presenting them with such a sophisticated tool of communication and leaving them to work it out for themselves.

It's pointless lecturing teenagers about drugs and sex, but there's no reason why you can't discuss these things. Let such chats be triggered by things you hear on the radio or see on the television together.

back in the real world

They say every man is the king of his own castle. But a king can always delegate or abdicate if he realizes he is incompetent. A dad can do neither!

Every dad needs to recognize and seize the right moment to sit down with his child and talk about…sex. It can either be awkward and embarrassing or factual, fun and instructive. Be prepared.

Any father hoping his child will go off to college should back up his own desire by ensuring it will be financially viable. This means putting into action very early on a financial plan that is likely to provide sufficient funds when the time comes.

Dads can help their children to learn about themselves and make sense of their world. This can have a profound and lasting effect on their social, emotional and intellectual development.

Create a suggestion box where members of the family can post ideas, desires, wishes and frustrations anonymously! Take turns reading them out at a family dinner every Friday.

Prior to each Christmas, teach your children to be caring and charitable. Help them to select and donate old toys they no longer love to help bring some Christmas cheer to other less fortunate children.

Think about starting a savings plan for your children. Consider how expensive home deposits, cars, holidays and weddings will be when they get older. It needn't be a huge amount put aside monthly, as over the long-term it will grow into a sizeable amount and will provide them with a great, secure start to their own adult life.

Take out a life insurance policy and a health insurance plan.

Search out whatever benefits you may be entitled to as a family.

Now you are a dad, it's time to take stock of your own wellbeing. Try to get fit and break a few bad habits such as smoking and drinking too much. Make a new start and you'll be there fit and healthy to play with and nurture your children for many years to come.

Set yourself the task of doing something positive to clear up all your debts to ensure that you leave no financial potholes behind for your children to fall into.

Help your child to understand charity by becoming actively involved yourself. Sponsor a child in an impoverished nation or help with collections or fundraising events for a chosen charity.

Don't be afraid to let parenthood take you outside your comfort zone from time to time.

Now is the time to make an effort to either make the house you are in the home of your dreams or to buy the one that is.

Do find ways to spend quality time with your children. Make all time with them Quality Time.

Parenthood is a great time to meet new people and develop new friendships. This is also a wonderful example to set to your children as they see you mix with other sexes, cultures, religions and races.

Parenthood is a perfect time to mend fences with relatives you may have avoided communicating with for years. After all, you want to set a good example for your children to keep in touch with you when you are older – so get on the phone and call those aged parents, siblings, aunts and uncles.

Take up meditation – it will help you keep your cool when dealing with tantrums.

Do find ways to balance your home life and your work.

Perhaps having a new child in your family will provide the motivation to enhance your professional career by seeking a new job and leaving a dead-end one behind.

If you are a dad who does not teach his children their duties, then you must be prepared to be equally responsible when your children neglect theirs.

Our children cannot be expected to understand the stresses of a working day. When you come home they will always be excited and want to play with you and get your attention. Never reject these moments – leave your bad day outside for a few wonderful moments with those who love you inside.

It's still possible to be the greatest dad in the world whether you live with your children all of the time or only some of the time. Use everything available to you to make them feel wanted and loved. They will respect you even more if you are supportive of their mother rather than making them choose between you.

Inspire other fathers with all the good things that you do for your own children.

Every parent should take heed of what it is that kids say they want and expect from their fathers. Much of it will seem familiar from your own childhood. Other things will come as a shock and wake up call to take action and instigate change in your approach to parenting.

Ask any child what they would wish from their father and most will say that they wish they could do more things together.

I once read somewhere that an extremely high percentage of children who were asked what they would like their fathers to do with them said they simply wanted them to sit and talk!

Who better than a father to help a girl feel good about being female? If your daughter sees that you enjoy her company and hearing what she has to say, it will be a tremendous boost to her confidence.

Why do fathers shy away from spending time with their daughters? After all, dads are the first men they will ever know.

A father spends his days trying to turn his little girl into a little woman. And when she does become a woman he spends the rest of his days turning her back into his little girl again.

By showing a daughter that you care for her and respect her you will also help her to understand the way she should expect men to treat her when she grows up.

Comfort them. Children, even tiny babies, often get a special feeling of security from being comforted by their dads when they are frightened or upset.

Don't push your children into doing things you wanted to do and missed out on. They need to live their own lives.

Show your love in different ways – tell your children you love them, take them fishing, go for a walk in the park, help them with their homework, and cheer them on at a school event.

What matters most for children is how you are with them as a dad. Even if you are not a full-time dad, your children need to know that you care about them and that, no matter what, you will look after them.

If you and your partner no longer live together try and work together to give your children the love and security they need, and they will grow up loving you both for it.

Give your children the greatest gift anyone could give another person – let them see that you believe in them.

Celebrate achievements no matter how small or insignificant they may seem – everybody prefers praise to putdowns.

Actively participate! Get involved in out-of-home activities, such as playgroups and parent/teacher evenings, or dive in at the deep end and set such things up where they don't exist.

Buy a little treat each week and put it on display. It is the reward for whoever gets up on collection day and puts out the bins, for example...you'll never have to do it again.

Make chores fun. Show how clearing the table and sharing with the washing-up after dinner can help create more time for a fun family game...something to look forward to.

Learn to illustrate to your child how a little bit of effort and application can lead to the glittering prizes in life – they will soon get the message and set their goals a little higher.

Expect your children to do their best and be proud of them when they do. Remember also to be proud of them when they try, but fail.

Set a great example by showing how keen you are to tidy up after yourself and soon youngsters will follow suit. If you do theirs jobs for them, they will always expect that to be the case.

Ignore all you've heard about the horrors of teen years. Instead, acquaint yourself with the facts a dad needs to know to be a successful father to a teenager – and be prepared for anything that might crop up.

Teen years are an important rite of passage we all go through – ignore them at your peril. Every dad should think back to his own youth and remember all those moments of importance and their significance.

Be there for your children at every important crossroad during their childhood and you will ensure a good and lasting relationship with them for the future.

Every dad has to learn to understand how important his teenager's friends are to him. Never criticize a friend in front of your teen or he will invariably take the friend's side.

It's good to know who your teenager's friends are. Make the effort to get to know them on first name terms, and perhaps even their parents.

Understand fully that an essential part of every teenage experience is a greater level of independence. Give graciously.

Be prepared to accept that for quite some time, your teenagers' friends are going to become as important to them as their own parents and family.

Design a table of pocket money jobs around the home for your children, with a varying scale of payment for the 'work'. Putting out the bins might, for example, earn them a third of what they would earn by washing the car.

All we can ever hope to ensure is that our children are aware of the importance of having good and dependable friends, and that with our help and encouragement, they might fall in with the right crowd.

Our children can have lots of friends in their life, but there will only ever be one dad. So, strive to enhance your friendship with them – don't alienate them or distance yourself.

Spend some time getting to know your teenage children and they may just open the door a little and let you into their world.

Adolescent life is a struggle for anybody. Don't be the thing that makes it worse for your child.

When we were children, most of us had friends we really envied because their homes were more 'teen welcoming' than our own! Find out what would make yours the coolest hangout for your teens and their friends.

As a dad, don't shy away from the matter of drugs with your teenager – remember, an ounce of prevention is worth more than a pound of cure.

Not all of us can be with our teens directly after they finish school each day so try to keep in touch by phone, by leaving written messages for each other or by meeting up online. Find things that will keep them pleasantly occupied until you reunite each evening, so that they are not left to their own devices.

Time alone and boredom lead to hanging out and open the gate to the risk of drugs. Help your teen to make the most of free time by encouraging extra-curricular activities that can help him find his identity in a constructive or creative way.

Work together with your kids and become a dad not to be feared but one who is happy to step in and help out.

Connect with your teen by doing things together. Make it part of your daily or weekly routine and it will become something you both look forward to.

Don't allow any hang-ups you may be carrying to influence your teenager in a negative way. Let them see that it is good to let go and move on.

No dad worth his salt would tell his children how to live their lives. He lives his life and lets his children live theirs alongside him.

Why are dads most often angry when their children are being most like them?

Don't leave your child in the position of having to say, 'Dad taught me everything I know. Unfortunately, he didn't teach me everything he knew!'

Dads should stay attached to their children at whatever cost. Even the smallest gesture of loving connection each day will keep the relationship a close one.

It is important that every dad values their children not by the qualities he wishes they had, but by acknowledging and respecting the qualities they do possess.

Try to avoid becoming the 'cop' in your kid's life – work with your child to provide discipline cooperatively. Agree between you what is reasonable and the sorts of penalties to be expected for not toeing the line.

Let your children see that even adults sometimes feel lonely, vulnerable or afraid. Don't be ashamed to let them see you shed a tear or are in need of a hug from time to time. Only by expressing these feelings yourself will you win their trust to express theirs to you.

Some dads tend to be in a rush for their child to try something they perhaps did themselves when they were younger. Slow down dad! If your child isn't yet ready, she will be all too soon.

Many fathers carry the memories of being teased or mistreated by their own fathers because they were a disappointment to them. Dads must avoid repeating the same mistakes with their own children.

When children reach their teens, their dads become their closest role model. Wouldn't it be good if your teen never had to worry about their dad acting irresponsibly?

Make
your paternal
project triangle

TOGETHERNESS
QUALITY TIME
AND FUN

surviving the empty nest

Just because the kids have flown the coop doesn't mean the fun has to stop. Get on that computer and play a game or two! Then challenge them to a game online for an hour now and then!

With the children gone it's time to refocus on your relationship with your partner. There are now things you can do together that you no longer need to stifle or lock the doors for!

Make preparations to ensure that family reunions and holidays are fun-filled and as exciting as the childhood years.

If you found through fatherhood that your vocation lays in inspiring young people, why not become a youth club leader.

When the kids leave home you become free to explore the world and re-discover its wonders.

A great dad is someone who let his kids try to find their own way, even though it can be painful to see them get hurt along the way.

Skating, swimming, skiing, surfing, cycling...these things don't have to end just because you don't have any kids in tow.

Now's the time to sort through the pictures and photographs...compile the albums and copy the videos onto DVDs and send copies to everyone to enjoy.

Don't forget to keep the journal going...collate all the collected stories, events, mementos and photos from over the years ready for an opportunity to share them with your children's children when the time arises!

Now is the time to turn your attention back to friends who have been missing out on your time and affections.

When your children leave you in the empty nest phase of life it is truly a major change. The important thing is to view the change as positive.

You don't stop being a dad even when your children are no longer underfoot. The secret is to keep connected to them and make sure you keep in touch with each other regularly.

When the kids grow up and fly the nest it is the ideal time for dads who have been concentrating all their energies upon that role to refresh themselves and reclaim a little time for them. Take up a new pastime or sport, or return to one you dropped when you became a dad.

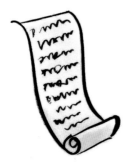

Make a list of all the things you have dreamed about doing, but could never get around to whilst being a full-time dad, and set about making them happen – some may even involve the kids when they visit home.

Enrol for evening classes and learn something absolutely new to you...from car mechanics to archaeology!

Try out a bungee jump – get photos to show your kids!

Be a hero dad and occasionally, and unexpectedly, send a parcel of nice things to your kids. A few treats will show you want to keep in touch and make them less homesick.

When the children have left home all your dad skills need to be turned, for a while at least, to the new vulnerable member of your family, who is inevitably going to go through a fairly emotional time…your partner.

A great dad is someone who held his kids when they cried and gave them the encouragement they needed to smile again.

A truly rich man is one whose children ran to fill his arms whenever his hands were empty.

Have a game plan in place for the moment your nest becomes empty. Having something lined up and in place can make the transition a quick and painless one, and your children will also benefit from not having to worry about you coping without them!

After almost two decades of taking things carefully and setting a good example for your children, now's the time to let your hair down – just make sure your insurance policy and will are in place!

Form your own band.

Consider joining a yoga class to keep that aging skeleton of yours supple.

Take your partner, or if single perhaps find a new one, on a world cruise. Send postcards to the children from each destination visited.

Design a den to replace the kid's playroom.

Try out an entire makeover – perhaps even enrol the services of a professional to help create an entire new image for you to enter the middle-age years. It will rekindle your own lust for life as well as satisfy your children's desire not to see you as a grumpy old man.

Take dancing lessons – anything from samba to Ceroc.

Relearn chopsticks on the piano.

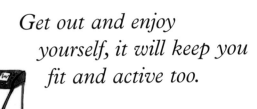

Get out and enjoy yourself, it will keep you fit and active too.

Take up skipping – it's fun and will do you good.

Now is the time to share your awareness and feelings with your partner and reflect on the childhoods you helped to create.

Enjoy the change around the home after the children have left – don't let it become a sad place. Instead, recognize that your home is positively papered with memories and fun, laughter and joy!

If your children are feeling lonely or homesick you could always link to each other's computers with an online camera so you can see each other as you speak...this way you'll all feel as though you are under the same roof.

Celebrate the fact that for the first time in decades your grocery bills are lower. Hooray!

Now you can go to the refrigerator and find there is still some food left to enjoy!

Now you'll be able to tell for certain just how untidy your brood was by just how tidy the house appears each day.

Please take note of how the house is covered in drying laundry far less often!

Get out more and travel. Even if you are alone there are so many companies offering group travel with people of your own age anywhere in the world at any time of the year!

It is not flesh and blood, but heart that makes us fathers and children.

Pour yourself a celebratory drink when the telephone bill arrives, as it will be a third of what it was when the kids were there.

Don't strip the nest entirely. Leave a few childhood toys and cuddly bears around where they can be seen by you to evoke memories of those early years.

Need more space for a project room, studio or office at home? No problem... box up the children's stuff and relocate it to the attic, but leave them a few mementos in a room they can always visit.

Enjoy the peace and lack of panic around your home and compare it to how things get each time your children visit you now.

Sling a hammock between two trees and laze the day away now that you have no pressures to provide a 24-hour taxi service.

Now, for the first time since the children were born you and your partner can make out on your own sofa any time of night or day without the worry of being discovered and having to explain!

You have the responsibility of making sure your kids don't spend their time worrying about you as a dad in an empty nest. Make the most of it.

Every kid wants his or her dad to realize his hopes and dreams for the future.

A great dad is someone who has been patient, helpful and strong for his children.

Every child wishes their dad to be in a good financial state when they leave home just as much as their dad wants to be able to ensure their financial wellbeing after they go!

Examine your calendar and admit that nowadays it is filled with far fewer parental tasks and duties. Ensure that the days are filled with rewarding activities including meeting up with your kids.

Every child should be allowed to feel welcome in their father's home, wherever it is and whenever they need to be there.

No dad should add pressure to their children's lives just because he feels the desire to be a grandfather.
Be patient.

What's that noise?
There is no noise.
Your home is QUIET!

Imagine, for the first time in years,
finding that there is hot water
when you want it! And
breakfast can be eaten
in peace.

Now you can have the
computer all to yourself and
use it whenever you want.

Make a plan with your children for when you are older, so they know your wishes should you become old and infirm and unable to cope alone. No dad wishes to become a burden on his offspring.

A great dad is someone who, although he scolded his kids when they broke the rules, always swelled with pride when they succeeded.

A great dad retained his constant faith in his children even when they failed.

A great dad is someone who picked up his kids after they fell, brushed them off, and let them try again.

Fatherhood teaches us that what we inherit from our fathers we have to learn all over again for ourselves so that it become ours – and so it shall be for our children and their children.

To be as good as our fathers we must be even better to our children than they were to us.

*Every dad should hold his head high,
as it doesn't matter to a child what
their father was – what matters is
who they will remember we were.*

*Being a good father is not
about slogging to leave a vast
inheritance for your children at
the cost of missing out on their
childhood – often the poorest
man leaves his children the
richest inheritance.*

A man knows when he is growing old because
he begins to look like his own father and sees
a memory of himself and his partner in the
faces of his daughters and sons.

Congratulate yourself for a job well done at raising your children! When you look in the mirror you will see their dad smiling back at you.

An Hachette Livre Company
First published in Great Britain in 2008 by MQ Publications,
a division of Octopus Publishing Company Ltd
2–4 Heron Quays, London E14 4JP
www.octopusbooks.co.uk

Distributed in the United States and Canada by
Hachette Book Group USA
237 Park Avenue, New York, NY10017

ISBN 13: 978-1-84601-263-1
ISBN 10: 1-84601-263-5

A CIP catalogue record of this book is available from the British Library

Printed and bound in China.

10 9 8 7 6 5 4 3 2 1